# Beyond the Sale – The Companion Guide for Real Estate Managers & Team Leaders

## Help Your Agents Create Great Businesses and Lives They Love

# Beyond the Sale–The Companion Guide for Real Estate Managers & Team Leaders

Help Your Agents Create Great Businesses

and Lives They Love

## by Ken Tutunjian & Jerri Udelson

Tremont Press
Boston

Select illustrations from Vecteezy.com.

**Beyond the Sale—the Companion Guide**
**for Real Estate Managers & Team Leaders:**
**Help Your Agents Create Great Businesses and Lives They Love**

Tutunjian, Ken and Udelson, Jerri, authors

Published in the United States of America. No part of this book may be used or reproduced without written permission, except for brief quotes excerpted for review purposes with attribution.

ISBN 978-0-578-46091-8

Cover and interior designs by Alex Hanna, invisiblecitydesigns.com

Dear Manager/Team Leader,

Thank you for purchasing *Beyond the Sale—the Companion Guide for Real Estate Managers & Team Leaders.*

This guide was written to help you work with your agents so that they can derive the most value from *Beyond the Sale—for Real Estate Agents: How to Create a Great Business and a Life You Love.* It summarizes the main concepts of the book and presents specific points to keep in mind as you review the material with them. It also provides an overview of the coaching process and coaching tips to help you engage in effective coaching conversations.

We hope that you will read the book and, if possible, complete the exercises. If you do, you will derive tremendous value for yourself and for your agency or team.

*We realize, however, that you have a very busy work life, and may not have the time or the inclination to do the exercises yourself. We recommend that (at the very least) you read through and become familiar with the material in this guide and in the book before coaching your agents on "Beyond the Sale."*

**Our goal in creating this guide was to make the process of coaching your agents as <u>easy</u> and as <u>effective</u> as possible.** We have provided key concepts for each chapter and restated the key takeaways from the book so that you are reminded of the main points of each section as you work with your agents. We have also provided a summary of core coaching competencies. Working with these competencies (e.g., coaching presence, powerful questioning, planning and goal setting) as you coach your agents will enhance your skills both as a manager and as a leader.

We hope you have a great time using the book and the guide. Coaching your agents and watching them obtain powerful and meaningful results is so gratifying. We can't wait to hear your success stories!

Best,

Ken and Jerri
TremontPress.com

# Contents

## *Part II:* Creating a Life You Love      39

## *Part III:* Tips from Top Producers: Seven Keys to Success      43

## *Conclusion*      51

## *Blueprint for Success*      53

## *Final Thoughts*      55

# Introduction

**This guide was designed for you to use when working with your agents on the exercises in** *Beyond the Sale—for Real Estate Agents: How to Create a Great Business and a Life You Love*. **It summarizes the main points of the book and provides specific points to keep in mind as you meet either one-on-one or in a group. The guide also includes an overview of the coaching process and coaching tips to help you engage in effective coaching conversations.**

## Why a Companion Guide?

*Beyond the Sale* is a <u>workbook,</u> not a novel. You can't just read the book and expect results, any more than you can read a cookbook and expect to have meals magically appear on the table. Agents need to read the book, complete the exercises, and follow through with the action steps they've designed to obtain the benefits.

Some people will do this, but many will just read the book and hope for the best. **However, if you create a <u>specific program</u> to work one-on-one or in group meetings with your agents, you can provide the time, motivation, and support for them to focus on the work and get the results they want.** This companion guide was written to assist you along the way.

## Premise of *Beyond The Sale*

**The premise of the book is that you can have a great business and a life you love once you become clear about what that looks like for you.** Readers move from identifying goals, to creating a plan to achieve them, to carrying out that plan.

*Beyond the Sale* contains a wealth of information, anecdotes and resources, but the most the important parts are the <u>exercises</u>. These enable the reader to determine

- What do I want? What's most important to me?
- What's missing from my business and from my life?
- What's worked for me in the past? What are my strengths?

- What am I actually willing to do to get the results I want?
- What specific actions do I want to take?

By reading the book and completing the exercises, the reader creates her own Blueprint for Success, **a unique <u>business plan</u> and <u>life plan</u>.**

**(Note: We have chosen to use "her" and "she" throughout the guide instead of "him/her," "he/she," or "them," since, according to the website of the National Association of Realtors®, "63% of all Realtors® are female.")**

## Structure of the Book

We designed <u>Part I, Creating a Great Business</u>, to be completed by the agent and then discussed with you, the manager or team leader, one-on-one. Part I can also be used in a small group setting with the manager, the agent, and her team.

<u>Part II, Creating a Life You Love</u>, is intended for the agent to complete on her own. It follows the same format and uses the same techniques as Part I to enable the agent to create life goals and an action plan for herself. Since the goals are highly personal, <u>we do not recommend</u> coaching your agents on Part II.

<u>Part III: Tips from Top Producers: Seven Keys to Success</u> is designed to be discussed either one-on-one or in a group format. Group sharing can be very valuable, as the insights and ideas of one agent can inspire, motivate and spur the creativity of other participants. We suggest that you hold a large group meeting weekly for seven weeks (or more) to review and discuss each key.

As a reminder, the seven keys are:
>**Key 1:** Provide Extraordinary Service
>**Key 2:** Maximize Your Time
>**Key 3:** Set Boundaries
>**Key 4:** Become Great at Delegating
>**Key 5:** Take Great Care of Yourself
>**Key 6:** Give Back
>**Key 7:** Express Gratefulness

# Before You Begin

Before you begin meeting with your agents, we suggest that you become familiar with *Beyond the Sale*. For the best results you will want to

- Read the book completely and then go back and do the exercises yourself.

- Set business objectives (pages 66-69) and marketing strategies
  (pages 71-73) for your agency or team.

- Complete the "Life Goals" exercises (pages 93-95 and 96-99) for yourself.

By actually working through the book and creating your own Blueprint for Success you will

- Understand the process on a deep level; and

- Create results for yourself and for your agency.

**Our goal in writing this guide is to make the process of coaching your agents as <u>easy</u> and as <u>effective</u> as possible.** In this guide we have provided

- <u>Key Concepts</u> for each chapter (e.g., values, purpose, goal-setting);

- <u>Key Takeaways</u> (e.g., *"Your values are the principles that are most
  important to you."*); and

- <u>Coaching Tips</u> to assist you in facilitating the conversations (e.g., "If the
  agent has articulated her values, you might then ask: *"In what areas
  of your life are you not living in accord with your values? Where are you
  out of alignment?"*).

## What Exactly is Coaching?

Coaching is a professional partnership with your agents. It is a *"thought-provoking and creative process that inspires them to maximize their personal and professional potential,"* according to the International Coach Federation. **It is not problem-solving and it is not therapy.**

In the book we have incorporated many of the tools and techniques of masterful coaches. These include curious inquiry, acknowledgment, values clarification, and forwarding the action (i.e., converting ideas into a plan and the plan into action).

## What are Powerful Questions?

**One of the most important skills of a coach is asking what are called "powerful questions."** These are open-ended questions that cannot be answered with a "yes" or a "no." (For example, *"What is the challenge here?" "What would it take for you to become fully committed to your goal?"*) Powerful questions are intended to evoke new perspectives for the agent. They often "stop the agent in her tracks," making her think before responding, and allowing her to discover new insights and solutions for herself.

The book has been designed to ask powerful questions (such as those above) and to guide the agent through a process of <u>self-discovery</u> so that she can reach answers on her own.

**COACHING TIP: HOW TO ASK POWERFUL QUESTIONS.**
Ask the question directly (for example, *"What's stopping you from taking that step?"*). The agent might not answer immediately. Allow her time to "sit" with the question. <u>Do not interrupt her or ask her another question</u>. Give her time to think.

**At this point you might become uncomfortable with the awkward silence. You might even want to jump in and help her answer the question.** (*Not a good idea!*) **<u>This is a time to practice becoming comfortable with your discomfort.</u> This skill will make you an even better coach.**

When the agent finally responds, <u>really listen to her</u>. Then ask follow-up questions, as appropriate (e.g, *"Tell me more about that." "What other actions could you take?"*). This process is at the heart of great coaching.

# Your Job As A Coach

**Your job is to support the agent, to listen actively—without judgment—and then to ask questions for clarification and to further the conversation— not to get the agent to arrive at the answer you think is best.** There is no "correct" answer.

> **COACHING TIP: THIS IS NOT PROBLEM SOLVING.**
> **It is perfectly acceptable for you to offer guidance, support, feedback and the wisdom garnered from your experience. However, the agent needs to do the work herself and come up with answers and a plan that will work for her.**
>
> Be wary of taking on an agent's issues or problems as your own. <u>Managers want to help, but often the best help is to listen and to ask questions—with genuine curiosity.</u> If the issue is beyond the scope of your job as manager or team leader (such as health or substance abuse issues or relationship or financial difficulties) you might suggest that the agent seek professional help. At this point you might also choose to suspend the coaching engagement and resume it at a later time.

(If you want to learn more about the coaching process we suggest you read *Co-Active Coaching, Fourth Edition: The Proven Framework for Transformative Conversations at Work and in Life* by Kimsey-House, et al. (2018).

Another good resource is *Coaching Questions: A Coach's Guide to Powerful Asking Skills* by Tony Stoltzfus (2008).

Also, the Appendix contains a list of the eleven core competencies developed by the International Coach Federation as well as a link to its website for more information.)

# Points to Consider as You Work with Your Agents

**Confidentiality** is a major factor in coaching. At the first session with the agent it is important that you tell her that the information shared in each of the sessions will be kept confidential.

**Privacy** for the agent is of utmost importance. In the book we ask the reader to *"dig deep"* and to answer the questions *"as honestly as you can."* In working with agents, we suggest that you ask the same of them. **However, do not ask them to share anything that they do not feel comfortable sharing. It is important to state this up front with your agents.**

**Disclosures** by agents. The answers to certain questions in the book (such as *"Where does your business come from?"* on p. 38) are ones that agents need to share with you, their manager/team leader, so that you can work on a business and marketing plan together. Answers to other questions (such as *"What negative, limiting beliefs do you have about yourself?"* on p. 25) are extremely personal. Your agents may not feel comfortable revealing answers to these and other such questions. **Encourage them to do the exercises completely and to answer the questions for themselves honestly.** Again, they do not need to share anything they do not feel comfortable sharing.

**Preparation** before meetings. Agents need to do the work on their own before meeting with you, as much as possible. They ought to come to the coaching or group meetings well prepared, bringing their completed answers to the exercises as well as any questions, insights and feedback they have. Of course, if they are stuck, you will have an opportunity to coach them during the sessions so that they can gain clarity and arrive at additional answers and insights.

**Scheduling.** It will be helpful to both you and your agents if you schedule coaching sessions at the same day and time each week or every other week. The meetings will then become a habit and the agent will be more likely to come prepared, if she knows that she has a coaching session every Tuesday at 3 PM, for example.

**Note-taking.** Take notes during the sessions, as appropriate. We suggest using a separate file folder or notebook for each agent or team. If there are ideas that you want to capture, goals that need to be remembered or follow-up homework, everything will be written in one place. **Do not, however, let your note-taking interfere with your being present for the agent.** A lot of information is conveyed by body language and tone of voice, as well as in the silences. **Be with the agent; you can make brief notes later on.**

<u>**Wrapping up.**</u> You may want to ask a reflective question at the end of each session. Some examples are: *"What three things did you get from this discussion?" "What are you going to do differently from now on?" "What would you like to add here?"*

These are just suggestions; asking questions at this time may or may not be appropriate. Use your judgment. There is no one "right way" to coach.

# Detailed Guide to
# *Beyond The Sale–For Real Estate Agents*

## Introduction to the Book - Pages 1-6

The introduction explains for whom *Beyond the Sale* was written and tells the reader how to get the most value from the book (pages 5-6). At this point the agent may or may not be committed to working through all of the exercises. That's okay. Encourage her to read through the book, and then go back and complete the exercises. There will be plenty of time later on to discuss her commitment to the work and perhaps, even to her career.

**Again, we strongly suggest that you ask the agents to do the work ahead of your coaching sessions and to come prepared to meet with you.**

## Agent Profiles - Pages 1-2

A good question to ask as you begin working together is: **With which of the six agent profiles on pages 1-2 do you identify?**

Some of the examples are: rainmaker, struggling "not-so-newcomer," and "lone ranger." The agent may immediately identify with one profile, or she may give a completely different answer. The question is designed to have her gain a broader perspective about herself and her relationship to her business. It is also designed to remind her that agents are in different places in their careers. **Ask the agent to check off or write her answer in the margin of the book on page 1 or 2.**

## To Get the Most Value - Pages 5-6

To get the most value from the book we ask the reader (on pages 5-6) to:

 1. **Set up a schedule** to read the book and complete the exercises. We recommend that you also schedule a series of coaching sessions with the agent

(perhaps weekly or biweekly). In our experience, sessions are typically 40 to 60 minutes long. If you are working with partners or with a team, allow extra time for longer sessions, most likely biweekly.

**COACHING TIP: BE DIRECT.**
Create a coaching schedule with her (and her team members) that all parties are willing to keep. Acknowledge at the outset that you understand that circumstances can change, and that sometimes either of you may have to reschedule a session. Stress the importance of honoring commitments to oneself as well as to others.

If the agent has not completed the exercises prior to the coaching session, you can either work on the questions together during the session or postpone the meeting until she has done the work on her own. If she hasn't even read the material, we advise postponing the meeting, or using that fact to discuss her personal commitment to herself and to her business. This can be a very useful and illuminating session for the agent—and for the manager!

**2. Take the CliftonStrengths® 34 assessment** (formerly called the Gallup Strengthsfinder 2.0) available at www.gallupstrengthscenter.com. This assessment was developed by the renowned Gallup Organization to help people discover their innate talents. It has been used worldwide by businesses, schools and community groups. It only takes about 20 minutes to complete, and the results can be very useful. They show the agent what she does best, so that she can build upon her strengths. The results of the CliftonStrengths® 34 assessment are used in an exercise in Chapter 3, pages 32-33.

**3. Gather data on her closed transactions** for the past year or two. These data are used to help the agent create her business and marketing plan, beginning with the exercises in Chapter 3, pages 35-39. If you are working with a newer agent, ask her to project ahead, and list her most likely sources of business and the areas in which she plans to focus. After she has been in business for a longer period of time she can redo these exercises and modify her plan accordingly.

**COACHING TIP: CLOSED TRANSACTIONS
ARE THE STARTING POINT.**

The agent might not know how to aggregate the data from the past year or two, or she might say that she doesn't have the time to do the work. Point out to her the value of knowing both <u>where her business has come from</u> (e.g., her top referral sources and her most effective marketing strategies) and the <u>specifics of her transactions</u> (e.g., average selling price, average commission, and the location of her transactions). These data are her starting point, and the information will be invaluable in helping her create a business and marketing plan going forward.

<u>NOTES:</u>

# Part I: Creating a Great Business

## Chapter 1: What Do You Want To Create?
**Pages 9-20**

## Key Concepts: Values, Purpose, Goal-Setting

- **Your values** are the principles that are most important to you. A fulfilling life is one lived in harmony with your values.

- **Your purpose** is what motivates and energizes you, what gives you the drive to succeed. It may change over time, as your needs change and your aspirations evolve.

- **Setting goals.** Before you can craft new goals for yourself, it is useful to see where you are right now. How close are you to your ideal life? In choosing goals for your business, make sure that they are specific, unambiguous, and measurable, and written in the present tense.

## Values: What Do You Stand For? - Pages 10-12

For some agents, the question *"What are your top three values?"* on page 12 will be very easy to answer. For others, it will be a challenge. Some people have never really thought about their values. They have never been asked to articulate them. This is an opportunity for agents to become clear about what is most important to them.

**COACHING TIP: LISTEN WELL.**
Your job during this session is to be a good and empathic listener. <u>Do not answer the question for the agent.</u> Encourage her to think about her values, about what matters most to her. She may become

uncomfortable if she does not have an immediate answer. <u>Make that okay.</u> You can also suggest that she review the examples of core values on page 11 and check off the ones that resonate the most with her. She can always come back to the exercise after she has had more time to ponder the question.

### COACHING TIP: DIG DEEPER.

<u>This is not a superficial exercise!</u> For some agents it can be a big awakening. After she has articulated her values, you might ask: *"In what areas of your life are you not living in accord with your values? Where are you out of alignment?"* If the answer is *"my health,"* for example, you might then ask, *"What is one step you can take this week to move toward a healthier life?"* If the answer is *"being creative,"* you might ask how she can be more creative in her work or at home with her family.

## Purpose: The Why - **Pages 12-14**

The exercise on page 14, *"What is your purpose?"* asks what is the agent's motivation for choosing a career in real estate. If she has lost motivation or feels burnt out, it is helpful for her to get in touch with <u>why</u> she is in business <u>right now</u>. As we say on page 13, *"Staying connected to (your purpose) will help you weather the ups and downs of this challenging profession."*

Some examples of purpose are: creating a business that will sustain the agent's family and ensure a legacy for her children; providing a vehicle for philanthropy in the community; and funding a lifestyle of travel and service abroad.

# Where Are You Right Now? - Pages 15-18

The exercise on page 15, *"Where are you right now?"* asks the agent to look at the current state of her business—her starting point.

The first question asked is ***"How much money did you make in the past 12 months?"*** As you well know, there is a lot of energy, both positive and negative, around the subject of money.

> **COACHING TIP: SET ASIDE JUDGMENT.**
> **Make it okay for the agent to be wherever she is right now—** whether it's having made $50,000 or $250,000 last year. There is no shame. This is her <u>starting point</u>, not her ending point.
>
> The agent may feel sad or disappointed as she realizes that she has fallen short of her goal. She may decide that she really doesn't want to do the work to get to where she says she wants to go. Or, she may be afraid of telling you the truth. It is important for you to work with her in a <u>non-judgmental</u> way. <u>You are helping her be honest with herself.</u> And by the end of the process her financial goal might change—as might her ideas about what she needs to do to reach this goal.
>
> It is also possible that the agent may not want to continue with the coaching at this point. She may need to take a break after having had some breakthroughs or major realizations during this process. <u>Make this all right</u> and invite her to return to the conversation in a month or two. She may need time to process everything she has learned about herself, and may want to do this work on her own.

The last question on page 17 is *"What are the biggest stressors in your life?"* Possible answers are:

Lack of money
Lack of sleep
Lack of support at home
Personal/relationship issues
Fear
Lack of personal time
Disorganization
Lack of support at work
Health issues
Worry.

**COACHING TIP: SUPPORT THE AGENT.**
It may be difficult for the agent to answer this question honestly. Yet, the answers can be very revealing. If the agent is stressed about debt, is not sleeping well, has no personal time or is very disorganized, the book can have a major positive impact on these stressors. Again, remind her that this is her <u>starting</u> point, not her <u>ending</u> point!

## Creating Goals For Your Business - Pages 18-19

On page 19 we ask the agent to create five goals for her business. These are <u>her</u> goals. She can write anything she wants, as long as the goals are <u>specific enough</u> so that she will know when she has reached them. If the agent wants to grow her business in a <u>non-traditional</u> way (e.g., not holding open houses on weekends, offering non-accompanied showings, marketing solely on social media), that's fine. These are <u>her</u> goals. If she doesn't want to grow her business, that's okay too.

**COACHING TIP: CLARIFY GOALS.**

**Your job is to help her clarify the goals she wants to create, without passing judgment on the goals themselves.** Just make sure that they are goals she <u>truly</u> wants, and that they are specific, unambiguous, realistic and measurable. Make sure that they are written in the present tense (for example, *"I am the go-to agent in the _____ neighborhood."*).

NOTES:

# Chapter 2: How to Create What You Want: Inner Actions
**Pages 21-30**

## Key Concepts: Self-Talk, Self-Belief, Visualization

- **Inner actions** are important in creating results.
- These consist of:
    - **Self-talk** - what you tell yourself, your internal dialogue
    - **Self-belief** - what you believe about yourself
    - **Visualization** - the detailed mental pictures you create of your goals.

- **You can change negative self-talk and self-beliefs** to new, positive intentions and beliefs which will support you in having what you want.

- **Visualization** is a great way to reinforce what you want. Creating a **vision board** can help bring your goals to life.

Chapter 2 is about taking **inner actions**, actions <u>in your mind</u>. These include what you tell yourself, what you believe about yourself, and the mental pictures you create of what you want to have happen in the future.

Chapters 3, 4, 5 and 6 are about taking **outer actions** – concrete steps <u>in the physical world</u>.

## Self-Talk and Self-Belief - Pages 21-26

Everyone has an <u>internal dialogue</u>, random thoughts that pop into one's mind on an ongoing basis (e.g., *"I'm not prepared." "I can't do this." "I'm going to fail."*). People also have <u>beliefs</u> about themselves that do not support them in creating the life they want (e.g., *"I can never have _____." "I'm not worthy of a happy life." "I'm intimidated by wealthy people."*).

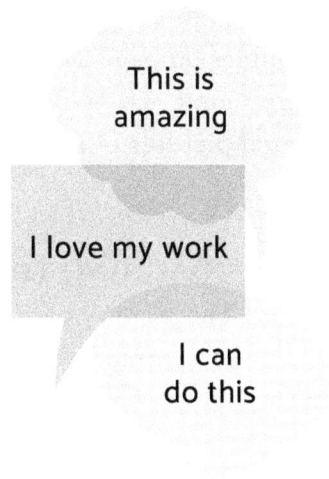

This is amazing

I love my work

I can do this

The exercises in Chapter 2 ask the agent to look at her negative self-talk and negative beliefs and to create new intentions and beliefs that support what she wants to create. (*"I can do this!" "I am prepared!" "This is going to be wonderful!" "I'm great at attracting new clients."*)

**COACHING TIP: HELP CREATE NEW BELIEFS.**
This can be a very powerful and transformative exercise. If the agent so chooses, help her look at her negative beliefs about herself. Make sure that she creates new beliefs. As you review the exercises with her, suggest that she post the new affirmations on sticky notes in places where she will see them daily.

There is a wonderful affirmation created by Marisa Peer, a British therapist: ***"I am enough."*** Peer has written a book, *I Am Enough: Mark Your Mirror and Change Your Life*, that is designed to help the reader increase her self-worth by using this affirmation and working with other powerful techniques. If you are coaching an agent who has issues with self-esteem, you might recommend that she read this book.

## Visualization - Pages 26-30

Finally, we discuss the concept of visualizing one's goals in one's mind, and provide several examples on page 27 to help the agent come up with her own mental pictures of her goals.

**COACHING TIP: CREATE A VISION BOARD.**
The vision board exercise is a great project to do with your agents as a group. It's a wonderful bonding exercise.

Below are some links to videos and pictures of completed vision boards.

https://www.youtube.com/watch?v=ohzH3FcwJos

https://www.oprah.com/own-oprahshow/oprah-surprises-ellen-degeneres-video

https://www.itwasonmyvisionboard.com/blog/archives/01-2015

http://www.hayhousevisionboard.com/?type=popular

NOTES:

# Overview of Chapters 3, 4, 5, and 6

These chapters are about taking <u>outer actions</u> – concrete steps in the physical world. Examples of outer actions are holding client appreciation events, asking for referrals, and creating an effective on-line presence.

## Chapter 3: How to Create What You Want: Outer Actions
**Pages 31-39**

## Key Concepts: Strengths, Sources of Business

> • Using your innate talents (those that you were born with or that come most naturally) is the best way to grow your business.
>
> • Building on what's worked in the past is also a key to business success.
>
> • Keeping track of the sources of your business will enable you to evaluate your sales, advertising and marketing efforts.

## CliftonStrengths® 34 Assessment - **Pages 31-34**

In Chapter 3 the agent looks at her innate strengths and talents (using the CliftonStrengths® 34 Assessment). **Encourage the agent to take the assessment.** It can be purchased at www.gallupstrengthscenter.com. It only takes about 20 minutes to complete, and the results can be quite illuminating, especially if the agent has doubts about her career choice.

Our experience has been that if none of the agent's top strengths involves <u>working with others</u> (as opposed to working with <u>things</u> or <u>ideas</u>), she is probably going to have a difficult time in this business.

**COACHING TIP: STRENGTHS ARE IMPORTANT.**
After taking the assessment, the agent may come to understand

herself on a deeper level. People often believe that the talents and skills that come most easily to them are "not a big deal," and that everyone has those same abilities. In reviewing her strengths, you might point out that the talents she takes for granted are actually <u>natural abilities</u> that she can focus on and develop to become even more successful in her career.

**COACHING TIP:**
**SUPPORT AND ACKNOWLEDGE THE AGENT.**
As you review the results of the assessment with her, make sure that you ask what the impact of discovering her top strengths has been on her. This is a great opportunity to acknowledge her talents and help her figure out how she will optimize these in her business.

## Where did Your Business Come From?

• The Numbers - **Pages 35-37**

• The Strategies and Sources - **Pages 38-39**

In Chapter 3 the agent looks at the specific sources of her past business (pages 35-37) and the marketing strategies she's been using that have been most successful (p. 38) and least successful (p. 39). The answers to these questions will be particularly useful as she moves forward and creates her Blueprint for Success. Make sure that she has completed both exercises.

<u>NOTES:</u>

# Chapter 4: It's All About Connection
**Pages 41-49**

## Key Concepts: Secret Agent, Lead Generation, Scripts, Fear

- Real estate is based upon relationships. You need to be engaged with people in your community to build a reputation.

- A number of technologies are available to assist you in lead generation and follow up.

- Scripts are a useful way to master specific conversations.

- Fear is a normal reaction to new, challenging situations. How you <u>respond</u> to fear is the issue, not the fear itself.

Relationships are at the heart of every real estate transaction. Chapter 4 discusses the <u>importance of connection</u>. In our experience, many agents are what we call "secret agents," agents who don't make it a practice of telling people what they do, and thus miss many business opportunities (page 42). In this chapter we also discuss lead generation technologies for "super prospecting" (pages 44-45), lead conversion services (page 45), and the importance of scripts (pages 45-46).

## Building Connections - Pages 41-44

**Encourage your agents to contact past customers, clients and referral sources** by visiting, phoning, writing, emailing, or texting, as appropriate for the client. These reconnections are easy and enjoyable, even for less outgoing agents, as one is strengthening an existing relationship. The agent has many reasons to get in touch— to update the client on recent neighborhood sales; to announce that a service guide to the area is now available; to invite the client to an event, to wish her happy birthday or happy holidays; or to commemorate the anniversary of his closing. Even if the agent just leaves a message, it will still be a reminder of the relationship.

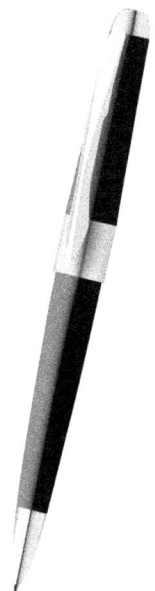

**COACHING TIP: ROLE PLAY AND GIVE FEEDBACK.**
Many agents are not comfortable in networking situations. If this is the case with an agent, suggest that she practice in small steps, role playing with you and other agents in the office. She can learn to make eye contact, to shake hands firmly and to make small talk.

Help her come up with a few topics (preferably not politics!) to talk about when she meets new people. **Make sure you give helpful, supportive feedback.**

You might also suggest that she attend networking events with another agent on her team or in the office. A great resource is *How to Work a Room, 25th Edition: The Ultimate Guide to Making Lasting Connections—in Person and Online* by Susan RoAne (2013).

## Let's Talk About Fear - Pages 46-49

What is the biggest barrier to cold calling and networking? FEAR. Fear of rejection, fear of failure, perhaps even fear of success. The discussion on pages 46-48 encourages the agent to face her fears and to take action anyway.

**COACHING TIP: CREATE AWARENESS.**
The exercise *"Looking at fear"* on pages 48-49 is a powerful one that you can do with the agent to help her deal with fearful situations. *(Hint: It's okay to feel fear. It can challenge you, motivate you and energize you. Just don't let it stop you. "Feel the fear and do it anyway.")*

**It is possible that the agent skipped over this exercise, not wanting to look at the feelings that fear brings up.** If she is fearful, talk with her, check in with her. Do the *"Looking at fear"* exercise together. Help her work through her fears. You can also sit with her or record her while she is making cold or warm calls and then give her <u>honest</u> and <u>supportive</u> feedback. Remind her that cold calls are "low stakes" situations. She will get better with practice and will develop self-confidence that will help her in higher stakes situations such as listing presentations and follow-up phone calls.

**If, on the other hand, the agent is fearless, let her go!**

<u>NOTES:</u>

# CHAPTER 5: Designing Creative Marketing Strategies That Work
## Pages 51-63

## Key Concepts: Market Yourself, Ask for Referrals, What Are You Willing to Do?

- There are many different ways to market yourself. You can
  - Expand your sphere of influence
  - Stay connected to past buyers and sellers
  - Ask for business—this includes referrals
  - Use social media.

- Keep your website relevant and timely.

- Develop and protect your brand.

- Get out of the office and talk to people. <u>Just do it!</u>

Chapter 5 presents a number of creative marketing strategies that work and that are used by top-producing agents. Many of them are designed to build a referral-based business for the agent; some use social media to acquire new clients.

**The most important action for the manager/team leader to take is to make sure that the agent has checked off the ideas that are <u>most appealing</u> to her.** She will be working with these strategies in Chapter 6 as she designs her own business and marketing plan.

<u>NOTES:</u>

# Chapter 6: Putting It All Together:
## Designing And Implementing Your Business and Marketing Plan
**Pages 65-79**

## Key Concepts: Business Goals and Objectives, Marketing Strategies, Action Steps, Deadlines, Budgeting

> • Your business goals, your strengths, your interests, and your past successes are the chief considerations when designing your business and marketing plan.
>
> • Marketing strategies need to include specific action steps (with deadlines) that you are committed to taking.
>
> • Create a system of reminders to ensure that you stay on track and meet your deadlines.
>
> • A detailed budget for your business should include marketing expenses and take into consideration your "draw," as well as federal, state, and other taxes and savings for retirement.

**This chapter is one of the most important in the book.** The exercises ask the agent to go back through her work in the previous chapters and create her own business and marketing plan. This plan is based on her goals for her business, what's worked for her in the past, and the creative marketing strategies that she is actually willing—and eager—to do.

## Creating Short-Term Business Objectives - Pages 66-69

## Creating a Marketing Plan - Pages 70-73

The agent is asked to create <u>three non-marketing objectives</u> (with specific action steps and deadlines) that she wants to implement within the next six months (pages 66-69) and <u>three long-term marketing strategies</u> (again, with specific action steps and deadlines) (pages 70-73) that she wants to undertake.

## Blueprint for Success - Pages 149-156

Once she's created her objectives and strategies, she's asked to copy them onto the Blueprint for Success on pages 149-156.

**COACHING TIP: ASK QUESTIONS.**

If the agent has not fully completed the exercises, you can assist her by reviewing her goals (p. 19), her business objectives (pp. 68-69), and her marketing strategies (pp. 72-73). **Ask open-ended questions to help her become clear.** Her goals should be <u>very specific</u> and the objectives and strategies <u>actionable</u> and <u>realistic</u>. It is perfectly fine if the goals are a stretch for the agent, but they should have a basis in reality. Goals such as *"I am making $500,000"* and *"I am featured in the New York Times business section"* are not realistic for most newer agents.

**COACHING TIP: "WANT" VS. "SHOULD."**
**Make sure that the business plan is something the agent is looking forward to implementing, and not something that she thinks she "should" do.**

**COACHING TIP: ACKNOWLEDGMENT.**
When she has completed the Blueprint, congratulate her. **This is a big accomplishment!**

<u>NOTES:</u>

# Chapter 7: Guiding Principles: Commitment, Accountability, and Legal and Ethical Standards
**Pages 81-88**

## Key Concepts: Commitment, Accountability, Ethical Behavior

- **Commitment** has great power. It keeps you motivated and focused on your goals.

- Different people respond to inner and outer commitments and expectations differently. Being **accountable** to someone else can help you stay on track.

- It is important to conduct yourself and your business in a **legal** and **ethical** manner, holding yourself to the highest possible standards. Periodically review federal and state laws and regulations and the NAR Code of Ethics and Standards of Practice to stay up-to-date.

## Your Commitment - Page 83

Chapter 7 presents guiding principles by which agents should operate. The exercise on page 83 asks the agent to look at her level of commitment to both her goals and to the action steps she has outlined.

**COACHING TIP: ASK ABOUT COMMITMENT.**
The question on page 83, *"What would it take for you to become fully committed (if you are not already)?"* is an important one and can provoke a useful discussion with an agent who may be holding herself back in her career and also, perhaps, in other areas of her life.

## Accountability - Page 83-86

This discussion references research by author Gretchen Rubin on the "four tendencies"—how different people respond to inner and outer expectations. **Encourage your agents to take the short (free) "four tendencies quiz" online at Quiz.GretchenRubin.com.** We encourage you to take the test yourself.

Coaching a "rebel" agent (who resists all expectations) can be very different from coaching an "upholder" (who responds readily to both inner and outer expectations). If you want to learn more about the four tendencies, you can read Rubin's book, *The Four Tendencies: The Indispensable Personality Profiles That Reveal How to Make Your Life Better (and Other People's Lives Better, Too)* (2017).

## Legal and Ethical Standards - Pages 86-87

This section provides an overview of legal and ethical standards, including the RESPA Act of 1974. We suggest that you supplement the material with state-specific rules and regulations, as well as updated Federal regulations and the NAR Code of Ethics and Standards of Practice, as they become available.

NOTES:

# Part II: Creating a Life You Love

**Part II, Creating a Life You Love, is designed to remind the agent that there is more to life than work!**

As stated in the Introduction, this Part follows the same format as Part I and uses the techniques introduced there to enable the agent to create life goals and an action plan for herself.

> **COACHING TIP: CLIENT PRIVACY IS PARAMOUNT.**
> Since these goals are highly personal, we <u>do not recommend</u> that you coach your agents on this section of the book. Of course, if the agent has questions or wants to share something personal with you, you always have the option to review the material with her.

That being said, we offer a few notes on Chapters 8 and 9 below.

## Chapter 8: How to Create A Life You Love
**Pages 91-100**

## Key Concepts: Life Goals, Action Plan

- Real estate should not be a substitute for a full, satisfying life.

- Become clear on what you want in your non-work life.
  This is key to creating a life you love.

- To create a life you love:
    - State your goals in the present tense;
    - Visualize what your life looks and feels like when you have achieved each goal; and
    - Create an action plan with action steps, deadlines and a budget, as appropriate.

# Creating Life Goals and an Action Plan - **Pages 93-99**

In this chapter the agent is asked to create life goals for herself (pages 93-95) and then to devise an action plan (including deadlines and a budget) for achieving these goals (pages 96-99). Specifically, in the exercise *"Creating life goals"* on pages 93 and 94 she is asked to rate her level of satisfaction with seven different areas of her life (e.g., friends and family, personal growth and health). She is then asked to choose which areas she would like to focus on, and to write goals for each area. For example, if her level of satisfaction with "fun, play and recreation" is rated 2 out of 10, she might create a goal of taking an improv class or playing tennis once a week.

The process and techniques for working with life goals are the same as those for working with business goals in Part I: Become clear about what you want, visualize yourself as having achieved each goal (i.e., what does it <u>feel</u> like, what are you <u>doing</u> as you are accomplishing each goal?), and then create a specific action plan.

> **COACHING TIP: REVIEW GOALS AND ACTION STEPS.**
> If the agent wants to review this chapter with you, make sure that she chooses goals that she really wants, ones that are specific, unambiguous, and measurable. Also make sure that the action steps are logical and the deadlines realistic. Choosing a goal of visiting Paris during the agent's busiest selling season, for example, may not be realistic.

<u>NOTES:</u>

# (Optional) Chapter 9: How To Create an Intimate Relationship
**Pages 101-107**

## Key Concepts: Commitment, Visualization, New Actions

- Creating an intimate relationship uses the same techniques you've learned to create other goals.

- This requires a strong commitment to having a partner in your life, including making time and space for the relationship.

- To create a new and different result you need to take new and different actions.

**COACHING TIP: RESPECT THE AGENT.**
This optional chapter is written for agents who want to create an intimate relationship. **Agents may not want to share anything about this chapter with you, their manager or team leader. That's perfectly okay.** Encourage them to do the exercises, if that seems appropriate.

If an agent tells you that this is a very challenging area for her, one in which she has many unresolved emotional issues, you might recommend that she speak with a professional in addition to doing the exercises in the book.

NOTES:

# Part III: Tips From Top Producers
# Seven Keys to Success

The Seven Keys to Success in Part III can be discussed either one-on-one with an agent or in a group setting. The material and exercises are designed to help the agent expand upon what she is already doing, as well as offer new approaches, ideas and techniques that are proven, powerful and effective.

## Overview

**Keys 1 through 4** (<u>Provide Extraordinary Service</u>, <u>Maximize Your Time</u>, <u>Set Boundaries</u>, and <u>Become Great at Delegating</u>) focus on the agent, her ways of working, and her relationships with her clients.

**Key 5,** <u>Take Great Care of Yourself</u>, is about self-care.

**Key 6,** <u>Give Back</u>, takes the agent beyond herself to the greater community.

**Key 7,** <u>Express Gratefulness</u>, offers the agent a greater perspective on her life and on what's most important to her.

**The value in working with the Keys in a larger group setting is that sharing ideas within the group can inspire, motivate and spur the creativity of all of the participants.**

**COACHING TIP: WORK IN TRIADS.**
If you have a large number of agents at a meeting, one way to organize the session is for the leader to present the topic of the day, to summarize the highlights (you can go over the key takeaways, for example), and then to break the large group into triads. Have people share their insights, ideas and perhaps even answers to some of the questions (again, as appropriate) within their triad, and then have a member of each triad report back to the larger group.

We suggest that you have at least one meeting to cover each key. The keys on
<u>Maximizing Your Time</u> (Key 2) and <u>Taking Great Care of Yourself</u> (Key 5)
can each be covered over two sessions. Self-management (getting organized,
becoming more productive) and self-care (especially getting enough sleep!) are
<u>huge</u> topics and major stumbling blocks for many agents.

★ ★ ★ ★ ★

## KEY 1: Provide Extraordinary Service - Pages 111-114

## Key Concepts:
The Client Experience, Going Beyond Expectations, Enhancing Service

- Providing extraordinary service means exceeding expectations.

- Hard work, focus and drive are hallmarks of the top producer.
  So are knowledge, expertise, generosity, and attention to detail.

<u>NOTES:</u>

# KEY 2: Maximize Your Time - Pages 115-118

## Key concepts:
Activity Versus Productivity, Time Blocking, Internal Prime Time

- Being busy is not the same thing as being productive.

- Spend your time on the activities that will have the biggest impact on your business.

- Block off time periods in your schedule for uninterrupted work requiring sustained concentration.

- Create systems and use checklists to stay on top of everything.

- Limit your time on personal social media and restrict your work-related social media to effective, non-controversial communication that is targeted in message and audience.

NOTES:

# KEY 3: Set Boundaries - Pages 119-123

## Key Concepts:
Time and Task Boundaries

- Set time boundaries with clients, customers, other agents and staff up front so that you are able to take time for yourself.

- Set task boundaries as well. Provide a list of resources to your clients so that you are not personally taking on tasks that are outside the scope of the real estate transaction.

## NOTES:

## KEY 4: Become Great At Delegating - Pages 124-129

## Key Concepts:
Delegating, Using Virtual Assistants, Growing a Team

- Learning to delegate is key to having a life.

- Do the things you are best at, and hire people to do the things they are best at.

- Use part time assistants, virtual assistants, and professional services to delegate tasks without hiring full time staff.

- Delegation is a process. Begin with the easiest tasks first.

- There are various models for growing a team or creating a partnership with another agent.

NOTES:

## KEY 5: Take Great Care of Yourself - Pages 130-135

## Key Concepts:
Self-Care, Sleep, Rituals

- Make self-care, especially your own good health, a top priority.

- Eat well, manage stress, and get enough sleep.

- Take time off!

NOTES:

# KEY 6: Give Back - Pages 136-137

## Key Concept:
The Joy of Giving

- Giving back is key to both happiness and success.

- There are countless ways to give back. Find a way that resonates with you.

- Give for the joy of giving, expecting nothing in return.

NOTES:

## KEY 7: Express Gratefulness - Pages 138-141

## Key Concepts:
Gratitude and Appreciation

- Expressing gratitude is about acknowledging and appreciating everything that you have in your life.

- Gratitude is the final step in the creation process. It brings more joy and positivity to your life and to the lives of those you touch.

NOTES:

# Conclusion
**Pages 143-146**

## Key Concepts: Reflection, Acknowledgment, and Celebration

The concluding chapter is an opportunity for the agent to <u>reflect</u> on her progress and for you both to <u>celebrate</u> the changes she's made and the results she's created since starting this work with you.

> **COACHING TIP:**
> **ACKNOWLEDGE AND CELEBRATE THE AGENT.**
> Make the tone of this session one of <u>celebration</u>. **The job of the manager/team leader is to acknowledge all of the work the agent has put into the book (and therefore, into her business and her life) and to offer useful feedback, honest insights, and sincere congratulations.**
>
> Too often, the agent will read a list of accomplishments as if it were a grocery list, without stopping to realize the magnitude and the implications of what she has just said. For example, *"I started exercising, I'm now working with three high-end buyers, and I just closed on _____."*
>
> She might even add, *"But I didn't get the listing on Pleasant Street, and I only went to the gym once last week."*
>
> It is your job as her coach to stop her and say, for example, *"<u>Wow!</u> Do you realize what you just said? You got two new referrals last week. <u>That's fantastic!</u> Remember, that was one of your goals—to build a referral-based business. Let's take a moment to celebrate that win."*
>
> As you go over the answers to the questions on pages 143 and 144, stop the agent after each response and give her a moment to let the "win" or insight sink it. <u>This is an important time for both you and the agent.</u> Also, thank her for her willingness to "dig deep" and to be present and honest with both herself and with you.

**COACHING TIP: RESPECT HER PRIVACY.**
The final questions on these pages ask the agent to modify or create new business and life goals, as well as to create goals for the next three and five years. We suggest that you ask the agent if she wants to review these with you, as she may prefer to keep them to herself. **As always, the decision to share is up to the agent.**

NOTES:

# Blueprint for Success

## Pages 149-156

The Blueprint for Success is the **culmination** of the agent's efforts. In the Blueprint she has outlined her values, her purpose and her strengths, as well as her business goals and objectives, her marketing strategies and action steps, with associated deadlines. Also, her life goals with specific action steps and deadlines have been created.

There are <u>three copies</u> of the Blueprint in the book, so that it can be updated periodically. We recommend that the agent review the material <u>yearly</u>, and update her goals and action steps as she sees fit.

NOTES:

# Final Thoughts

We love feedback! Please email us at info@TremontPress.com with your comments on the book and on this companion guide. We intend to update them both periodically, and your suggestions, ideas and notes are greatly appreciated.

Also, join our Facebook Group, Beyond the Sale—for Real Estate Agents and participate in the discussions with other managers, team leaders and agents.

Thank you so much for your participation.

Best,

Ken and Jerri

> "If we did all the things we are capable of,
> we would literally astound ourselves."
> —Thomas A. Edison

# Appendix: Coaching Competencies

The International Coach Federation has developed eleven core competencies that comprise the skills professional coaches need to have in order to become certified. These are:

### A. Setting the Foundation
1. Meeting Ethical Guidelines and Professional Standards
2. Establishing the Coaching Agreement

### B. Co-creating the Relationship
3. Establishing Trust and Intimacy with the Client
4. Coaching Presence

### C. Communicating Effectively
5. Active Listening
6. Powerful Questioning
7. Direct Communication

### D. Facilitating Learning and Results
8. Creating Awareness
9. Designing Actions
10. Planning and Goal Setting
11. Managing Progress and Accountability

You can read them in detail at https://coachfederation.org/core-competencies. You can practice working with these competencies and enhance your skills as a manager and as a coach by taking workshops or coach-specific training.

For purposes of this guide, we want to emphasize several of the above:

- Establishing trust and intimacy with the client – the ability to create a safe, supportive environment that produces ongoing mutual respect and trust.

- Coaching presence – the ability to be fully conscious and create a spontaneous relationship with the client.

- Communicating effectively – active listening, powerful questioning, and direction communication.

- <u>Facilitating learning and results</u> – creating awareness, designing actions, planning and goal setting, and managing progress and accountability.

Each of these competencies is discussed in detail in the document referenced above.

# Resources

**Books**

Kimsey-House, et al. *Co-Active Coaching, Fourth Edition: The Proven Framework for Transformative Conversations at Work and in Life.* Boston: Nicholas Brealey Publishing, 2018.

Peer, Marissa. *I Am Enough: Mark Your Mirror and Change Your Life.* Self-published, 2018.

RoAne, Susan. *How to Work a Room, 25th Edition: The Ultimate Guide to Making Lasting Connections—in Person and Online.* New York: William Morrow & Company, 2013.

Rubin, Gretchen, *The Four Tendencies: The Indispensable Personality Profiles That Reveal How to Make Your Life Better (and Other People's Lives Better, Too).* New York: Harmony Books, 2017.

Stoltzfus, Tony. *Coaching Questions: A Coach's Guide to Powerful Asking Skills.* Self-published, 2008.

**Assessments**

gallupstrengthscenter.com CliftonStrengths® 34 assessment
(formerly called the Gallup Strengthsfinder 2.0)

Quiz.GretchenRubin.com – Four Tendencies Quiz – How one responds to expectations

# Acknowledgments

Thank you so much to the wonderful managers who were early readers of this guide: John Angier, Marc Giroux, Janet Reilly and Thalia Tringo. Your input has been tremendously useful.

A special thanks to Marcia Polese for your invaluable edits and feedback.

To Alex Hanna: We so appreciate your brilliant cover and book designs. Gracias.

# About the Authors

**Ken Tutunjian** is the vice president and manager of the number one Coldwell Banker Residential Brokerage office in Massachusetts. He oversees more than 85 agents in the selling and renting of condominiums, townhouses and cooperatives in the luxury Boston market. His specialty is working with developers in the areas of historic renovation and mid-rise new construction.

Ken is recognized by the agents and staff he manages for his approachable, yet direct, style, and for his kindness and caring. As some of his agents have said, *"He has always been there for me." "He's perceptive and intuitive; he's not just a manager, he's an advisor and coach."*

Ken's motto is *"Giving back is in my DNA, and nurturing Boston is an honor."* He has been active on many local boards, including Community Servings (where he and his team raised nearly $90,000 to feed critically ill individuals in New England) and the Back Bay Association. Ken also serves as a city commissioner on the Back Bay Architectural Commission.

Ken is a classically trained musician and a former museum curator. He lives in Boston's South End.

**Jerri Udelson** has been called a "coaching pioneer and visionary." She is one of the first hundred people to be designated a Master Certified Coach by the International Coach Federation. Jerri is the founder of International Coaching Week, an annual worldwide event that educates the public about the value of working with a professional coach. Jerri was recently named a 2019 Real Estate Newsmaker—Thought Leader by RISMedia.

Her company, Entrepreneurial Coaching and Consulting, focuses on helping real estate agents, entrepreneurs and self-employed professionals grow their businesses quickly and strategically, while also creating lives they love.

Clients have called her *"direct and insightful," "terrific to work with," "very caring and intuitive,"* and *"warm, fun to talk to, and non-judgmental."*

Jerri holds a B.S. degree in psychology from Tufts University and a Master's degree in health services administration from Yale. Prior to starting her coaching business she was a real estate broker in Cambridge, MA, and the COO and CFO of a training company.

Jerri lives in Santa Fe, NM with her partner and their Siamese cats. She coaches worldwide, via phone, text and email.

www.ingramcontent.com/pod-product-compliance
Lightning Source LLC
Chambersburg PA
CBHW051352200326
41521CB00014B/2548